cho
col
ate

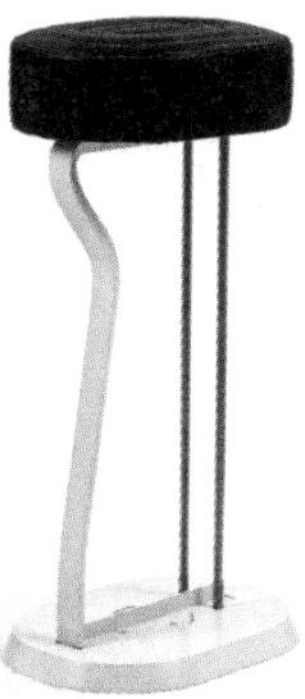

HATE!

2
CHARLES EAMES designed*
2 NEW CHAIRS
for dining
ARM & SIDE
upholstered
in
many
colors
at
LA
FONDA
DEL
SOL
RESTAURANT
1
1730-1 arm shell
side shell 1700-1
vinyl bound
*HERMAN MILLER, INC. ZEELAND, MICHIGAN

DANGER

DOWNTOWN

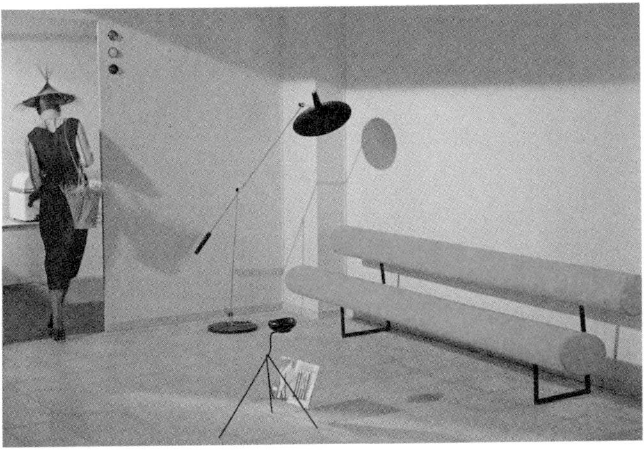

7·6335

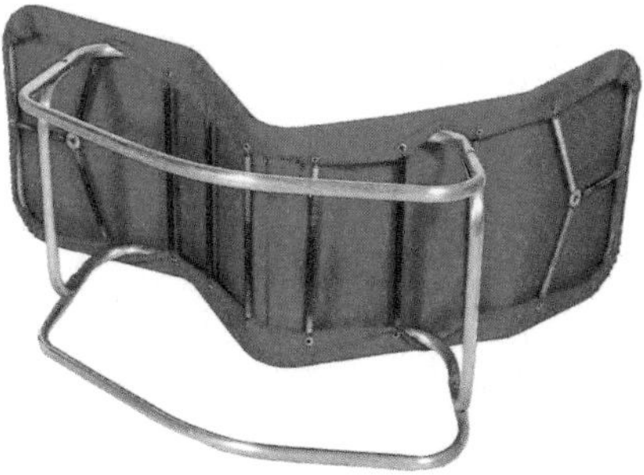

LA
1 0 1

RYZE

NO
PARKING

GIANTS

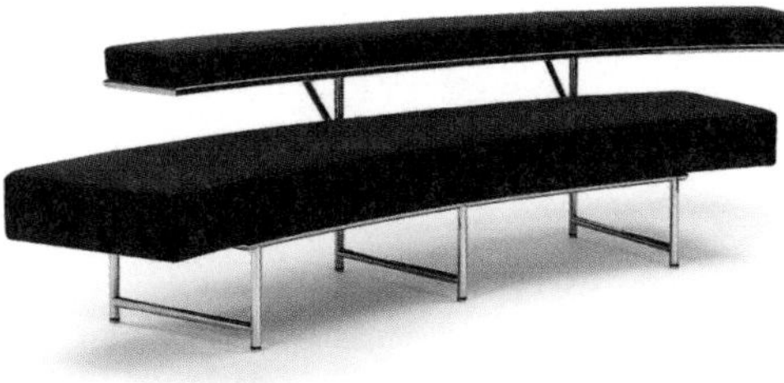

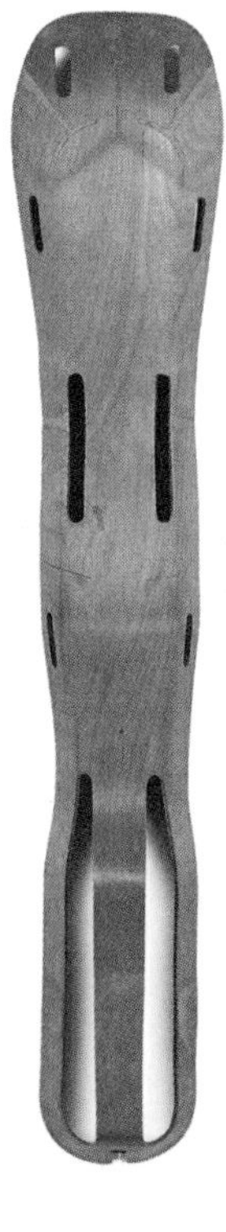

OOPS...
BOOM!
NATAS KAUPAS

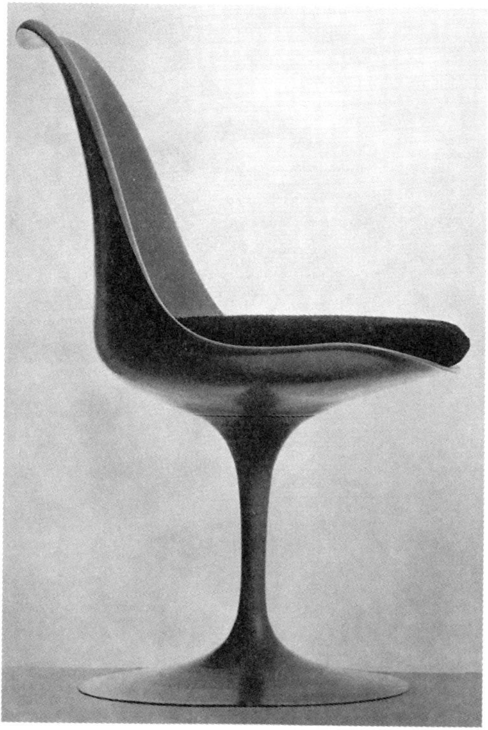

CHINO, SANE, JA, KET,

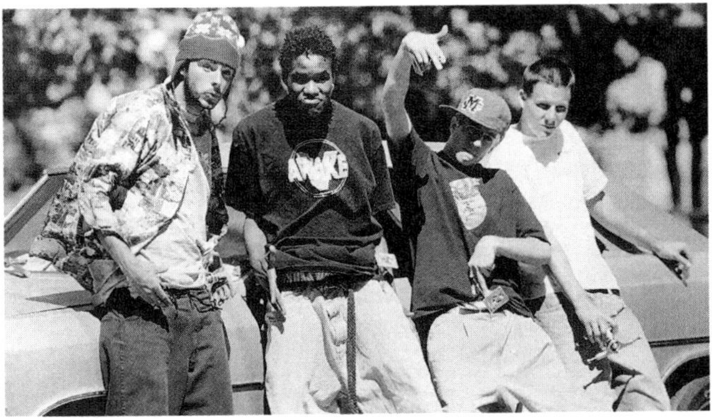
AWAKE

2020

Picture Credits

All reasonable efforts have been made to contact the copyright holders of the photographs used in this book. We apologize to anyone that we have been unable to reach.

Eames Office LLC (Page 26) • Estate of Scott Burton / Artist Rights Society (ARS) / Vitra Design Museum, Photo: Jürgen Hans (Page 40) • BD Barcelona (Page 12) • Bill Thomas (Page 11) • Courtesy of the Frances Loeb Library, Visual Collections, Harvard University Graduate School of Design, Image Credit: Serge Chermayeff, Ivan and Peter Chermayeff (Page 32) • Chocolate Skateboards (Page 1) • Craig Costello KR (Page 8) • Gabe Morford (Pages 5, 10) • Getty Images (Page 54) • Herman Miller (Pages 13, 36) • Miller House and Garden, Columbus, Indiana. Courtesy of Newfields. Miller House and Garden is owned and cared for by the Indianapolis Museum of Art at Newfields. Tours at Miller House and Garden are made possible through the Columbus Area Visitors Center (Page 16) • Ishod Wair (Page 15) • Janette Beckman (Page 31) • Jody Morris (Page 41) • Jody Morris / Thrasher Magazine (Page 46) • Jon Naar / Knoll (Page 2) • Knoll (Page 56) • Library of Congress, Prints & Photographs Division, Balthazar Korab Collection (Page 37) • Life / Getty Images (Page 6) • Manufacturer ClassiCon authorised by The World Licence Holder Aram Designs Ltd. (Pages 7, 27, 42) • Michael Miller (Page 25) • Post (Pages 20, 53, 59) • Albuquerque Museum, Gift of the Estate of Ralph and Clarabel Looney (Page 48) • Sean Dolinsky / Thrasher Magazine (Page 29) • Shane Aukland (Page 60) • Spectrum Design, BR 02 Sofabed by Martin Visser (Page 33) • Venture Trucks (Pages 49, 55) • Zanotta (Page 19)

Index

1 Keenan Milton
2 Francesca Breuer
3 Hush
4 Cantilever Model No. 26, Aalvar Aalto
5 Jahmal Williams
6 Eliot Noyes
7 Bar Stool No. 2, Eileen Gray
8 Ryze
9 Diesis, Antonio Citterio and Paolo Nava
10 EMB crew
11 Mike Carroll
12 Catalano, Oscar Tusquets Blanca and Lluís Clotet
13 La Fonda Chairs, Charles and Ray Eames
14 Set and JD
15 Ishod Wair
16 Miller House, Eero Saarinen and Alexander Girard
17 JA
18 Morrison and Hannah office seating, Andrew Morrison and Bruce Hannah
19 Sacco Chair, Piero Gatti, Cesare Paolini and Franco Teodoro
20 Post
21 Mike Carroll
22 Mrs. Arpel's sofa in Mon Oncle, Jacques Tati
23 SP, Sex and Sly
24 Barwa Chair, Edgar Bartolucci and John J. Waldheim
25 Eazy-E
26 Don Albinson and Charles Eames
27 Bar Stool No. 1, Eileen Gray
28 Ryze
29 Mike Carrol
30 Tongue chair, Arne Jacobsen
31 Gang Starr and posse
32 Chermayeff Studio, Serge Chermayeff
33 BR 02 sofa bed, Martin Visser
34 Guy Mariano
35 Ghost
36 Eames Office Seating, Charles and Ray Eames
37 Miller House, Eero Saarinen
38 Ryze
39 MQ
40 Soft Geometric Chair, Scott Burton
41 Guy Mariano
42 Monte Carlo, Eileen Gray
43 Leg Splint, Charles and Ray Eames
44 Natas Kaupas skateboard
45 No. 151 / Tulip Chair, Eero Saarinen
46 Eric Koston
47 Chino, Sane, JA and Ket
48 Georgia O'Keeffe, Abiquiu House
49 James Kelch, Jovontae Turner, Mike Carrol and Kelly Bird
50 Malator, Future Systems
51 Miller House, Eero Saarinen and Alexander Girard
52 Hamilton Harris
53 Post
54 Eero Saarinen
55 Mike Carroll
56 Morrison and Hannah office seating Andrew Morrison and Bruce Hannah
57 JD and Set
58 Jean Prouvé tables
59 Post
60 Cory Kennedy

Jonathan Olivares
Seeing

First Edition

First compiled for Extraperlo, curated by MC Didero
and Jorge Penadés, Madrid, February 2021

Published by Nieves
www.nievesbooks.com

ISBN 978-3-907179-49-9